WEAPONS AND EQUIPMENT

of the

NORTH KOREAN ARMY

1950

The Naval & Military Press Ltd

Published by the
The Naval & Military Press
in association with the Royal Armouries

Unit 10 Ridgewood Industrial Park,
Uckfield, East Sussex, TN22 5QE
Tel: +44 (0) 1825 749494
Fax: +44 (0) 1825 765701

MILITARY HISTORY AT YOUR FINGERTIPS
www.naval-military-press.com

ONLINE GENEALOGY RESEARCH
www.military-genealogy.com

ONLINE MILITARY CARTOGRAPHY
www.militarymaproom.com

The Library & Archives Department at the Royal Armouries Museum, Leeds, specialises in the history and development of armour and weapons from earliest times to the present day. Material relating to the development of artillery and modern fortifications is held at the Royal Armouries Museum, Fort Nelson.

For further information contact:
Royal Armouries Museum, Library, Armouries Drive,
Leeds, West Yorkshire LS10 1LT
Royal Armouries, Library, Fort Nelson, Down End Road, Fareham PO17 6AN

Or visit the Museum's website at
www.armouries.org.uk

In reprinting in facsimile from the original, any imperfections are inevitably reproduced and the quality may fall short of modern type and cartographic standards.

> **RESTRICTED**
>
> The information given in this document is not to be communicated, either directly or indirectly, to the Press or to any person not authorized to receive it.

WEAPONS AND EQUIPMENT

of the

NORTH KOREAN ARMY

M.I. 10
WAR OFFICE,
AUGUST 1950.

M.I. 10,
The War Office,
LONDON, S.W.1.

August, 1950

Weapons and Equipment of the North Korean Army

1. The object of this publication is to acquaint you with the appearance and characteristics of the weapons and equipment of the North Korean Army.

2. The weapons used by the North Korean Army are almost entirely of Russian pattern. Among the few exceptions so far noted are some Japanese and U.S. rifles used by guerillas. Use may be made of other equipment captured from the United Nations forces.

3. The illustrations which follow depict

    (a) equipments which have been positively identified or may with reasonable certainty be presumed to be in use by North Korean troops. The titles below the photographs of these equipments are starred.

    (b) other equipments which might well be used by the North Koreans.

4. All the equipment illustrated is of Russian pattern unless otherwise stated.

5. Tank Armour. The most heavily armoured portions of all Russian A.F.Vs. are the hull and turret front. Skirting plates to protect the tracks have not so far been used on any Russian tank in Korea.

I N D E X

7.62 mm.	Nagant Revolver M. 95
7.62 mm.	Tokarev Pistol M. 30 "T.T."
7.62 mm.	Mossin-Nagant Rifle M. 91/30
7.62 mm.	" " Carbine M. 38
7.62 mm.	" " " M. 44
7.62 mm.	Machine Carbine Model 41 "P.P.Sh."
7.62 mm.	" " " 43 "P.P.S."
7.62 mm.	Degtyarev L.M.G. DP.
7.62 mm.	Maxim M.M.G. M. 1910
7.62 mm.	Goryunov M.M.G. M 1943
12.7 mm.	Degtyarev M. 1938 H.M.G. "D Sh. K"
14.5 mm	Degtyarev Anti-Tank Rifle M. 41 "P.T.R.D."
14.5 mm.	Simonov " " " " " "P.T.R.S."
50 mm.	Mortar M. 40
82 mm.	" M. 37
82 mm.	" M. 41
82 mm.	" M. 43
120 mm.	" M. 38
Anti-Personnel Hand Grenade M. 14/30	
" " "R.G.D." Hand Grenade M. 33	
" " "F.1" Hand Grenade	
" " "R.G." Hand Grenade M. 41	
" " "R.T.D." " " M. 42	
Anti-Vehicle "R.P.G." Hand Grenade M. 40	
Anti-Tank "R.P.G." " " M. 43	
Anti-Tank "R.P.G.6" " "	

7.62 cm.	Infantry or Regimental Gun Model 27
" "	" " " " " " " 43
"	Mountain Gun " 38

7.62 cm. Field / Anti-Tank Gun   Model 42
12.2 cm. Field Howitzer   "   38
12.2 cm.   "   Gun   "   31/37
15.2 cm. Medium Gun Howitzer   "   37
15.2 cm.   "   Howitzer   "   38
15.2 cm.   "   "   "   43
4.5 cm. Anti-Tank Gun   Models 32 and 37
4.5 cm.   "   "   "   Model 42
5.7 cm.   "   "   "   "   41
5.7 cm.   "   "   "   "   43
25 mm. Anti-Aircraft Gun   "   40
37 mm.   "   "   "   "   39
76 mm.   "   "   "   "   38
85 mm.   "   "   "   "   39

Light Tank T. 70
Medium "   T. 34
  "   "   T. 34-85 (See also diagram at back)
Heavy   "   J.S.1
  "   "   J.S.2
  "   "   J.S.3   (See also diagram at back)
S.P. Gun   S.U.76
  "   "   S.U.85
  "   "   S.U.100
  "   "   J.S.U.122
  "   "   J.S.U.152
Armoured Car B.A. 10
   "   " B.A. 64

POMZ-2 Mine
TM-41
TMD-B
Japanese Type 93 Mine
   "   "   3   "
   "   Hemispherical Anti-Boat Mine Type 98.

STOP PRESS
160 mm. Mortar M. 43

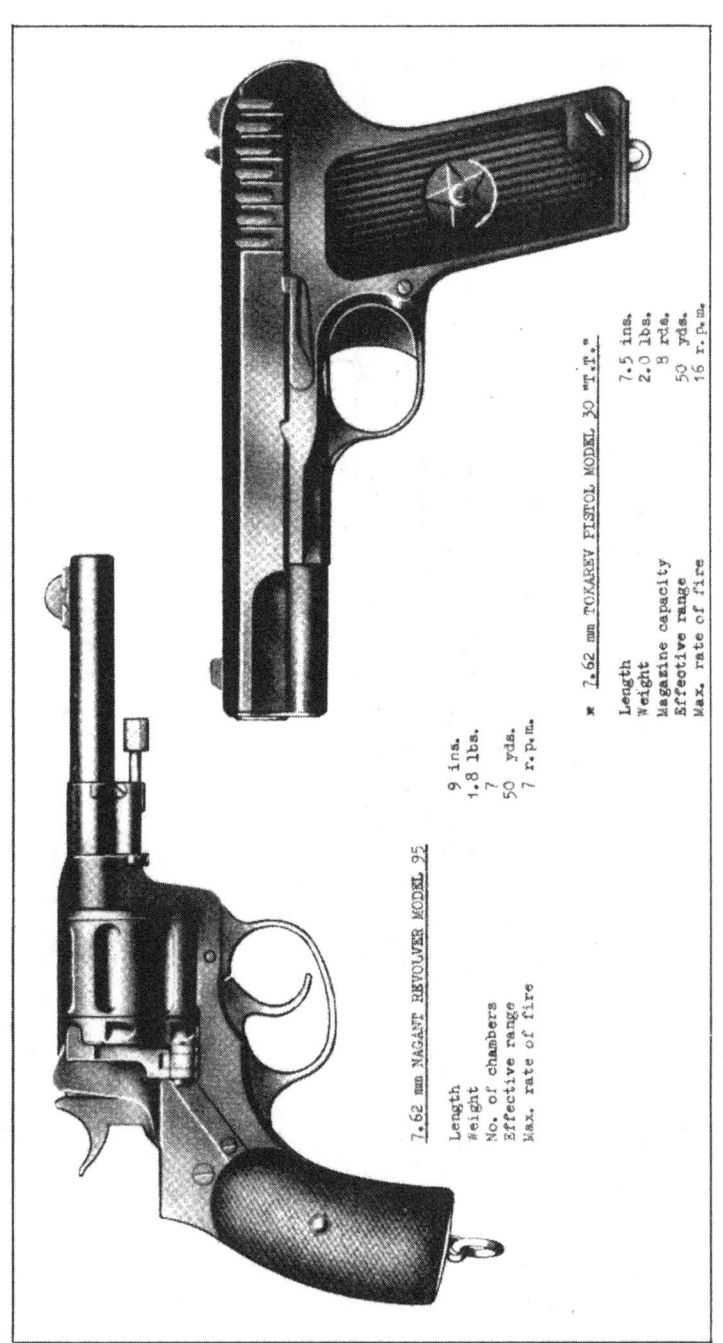

7.62 mm NAGANT REVOLVER MODEL 95

Length	9 ins.
Weight	1.8 lbs.
No. of chambers	7
Effective range	50 yds.
Max. rate of fire	7 r.p.m.

* 7.62 mm TOKAREV PISTOL MODEL 30 "T.T."

Length	7.5 ins.
Weight	2.0 lbs.
Magazine capacity	8 rds.
Effective range	50 yds.
Max. rate of fire	16 r.p.m.

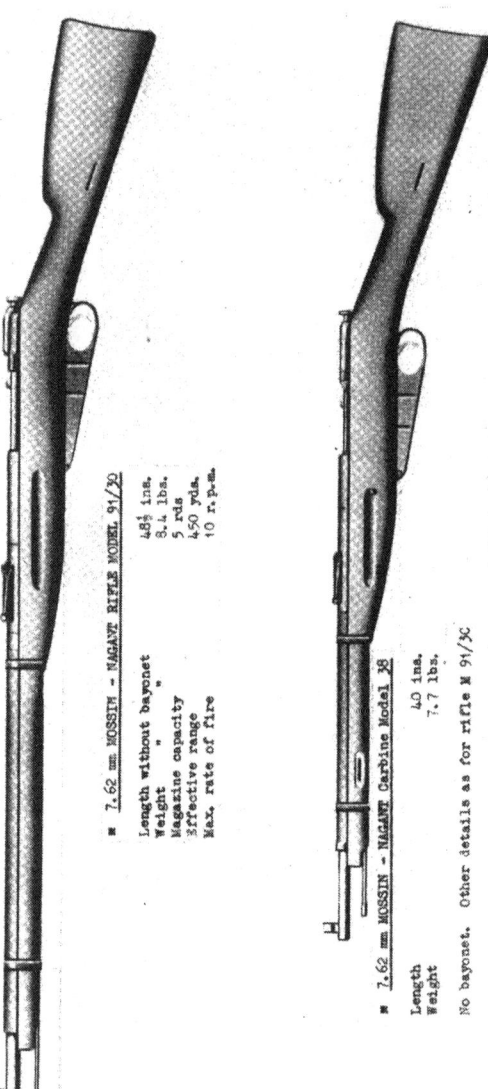

■ 7.62 mm MOSSIN - NAGANT RIFLE MODEL 91/30

Length without bayonet 48½ ins.
Weight   "   "   8.4 lbs.
Magazine capacity   5 rds
Effective range   450 yds.
Max. rate of fire   10 r.p.m.

■ 7.62 mm MOSSIN - NAGANT Carbine Model 38

Length 40 ins.
Weight 7.7 lbs.

No bayonet. Other details as for rifle M 91/30

■ 7.62 mm MOSSIN - NAGANT CARBINE Model 44

Length, Bayonet folded 40 ins.
   "   "   fixed   52 ins.
Weight   8.6 lbs.

Has permanently attached folding bayonet. Other details as for rifle M 91/30.

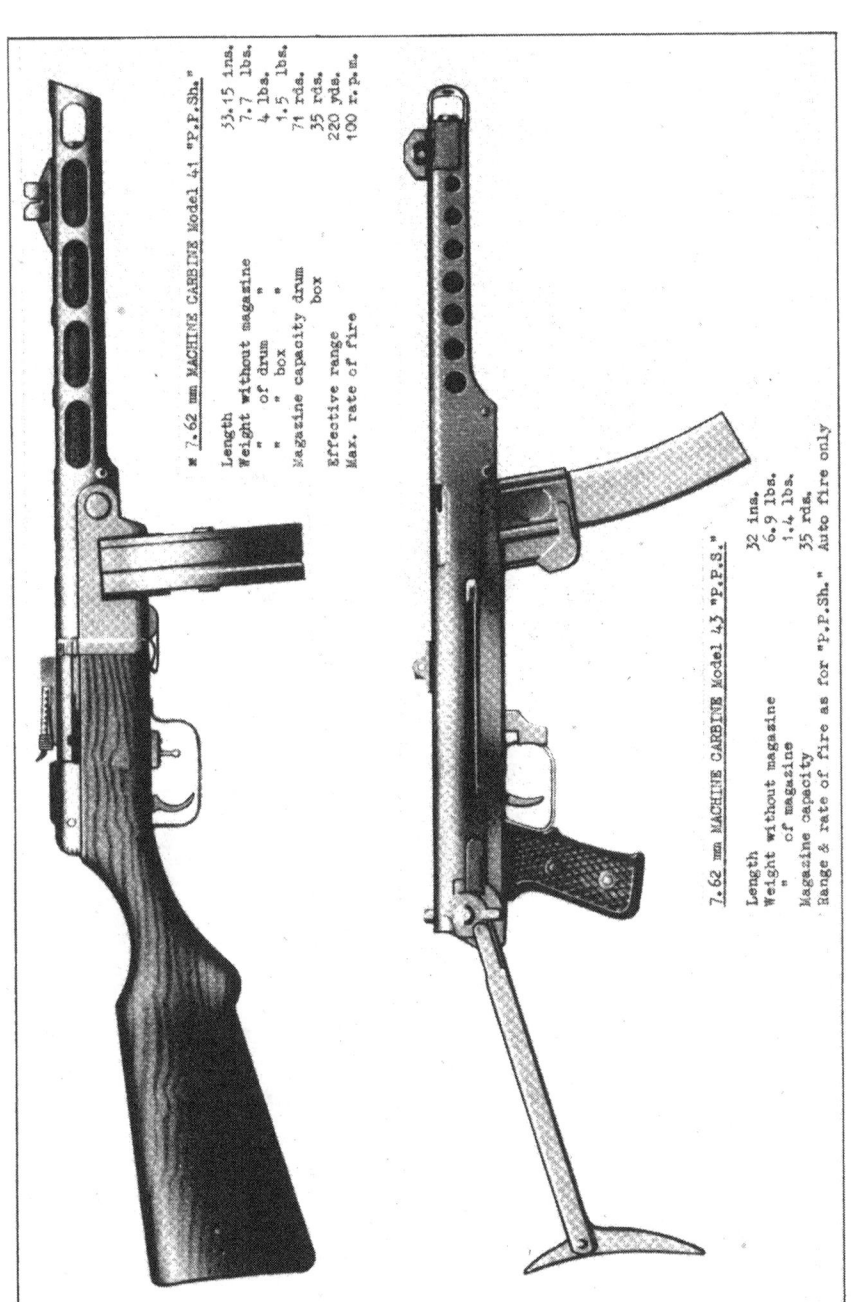

* 7.62 mm MACHINE CARBINE Model 41 "P.P.Sh."

Length   33.15 ins.
Weight without magazine   7.7 lbs.
   "   of drum   4 lbs.
   "   " box   1.5 lbs.
Magazine capacity drum   71 rds.
   "   "   box   35 rds.
Effective range   220 yds.
Max. rate of fire   100 r.p.m.

7.62 mm MACHINE CARBINE Model 43 "P.P.S."

Length   32 ins.
Weight without magazine   6.9 lbs.
   "   of magazine   1.4 lbs.
Magazine capacity   35 rds.
Range & rate of fire as for "P.P.Sh." Auto fire only

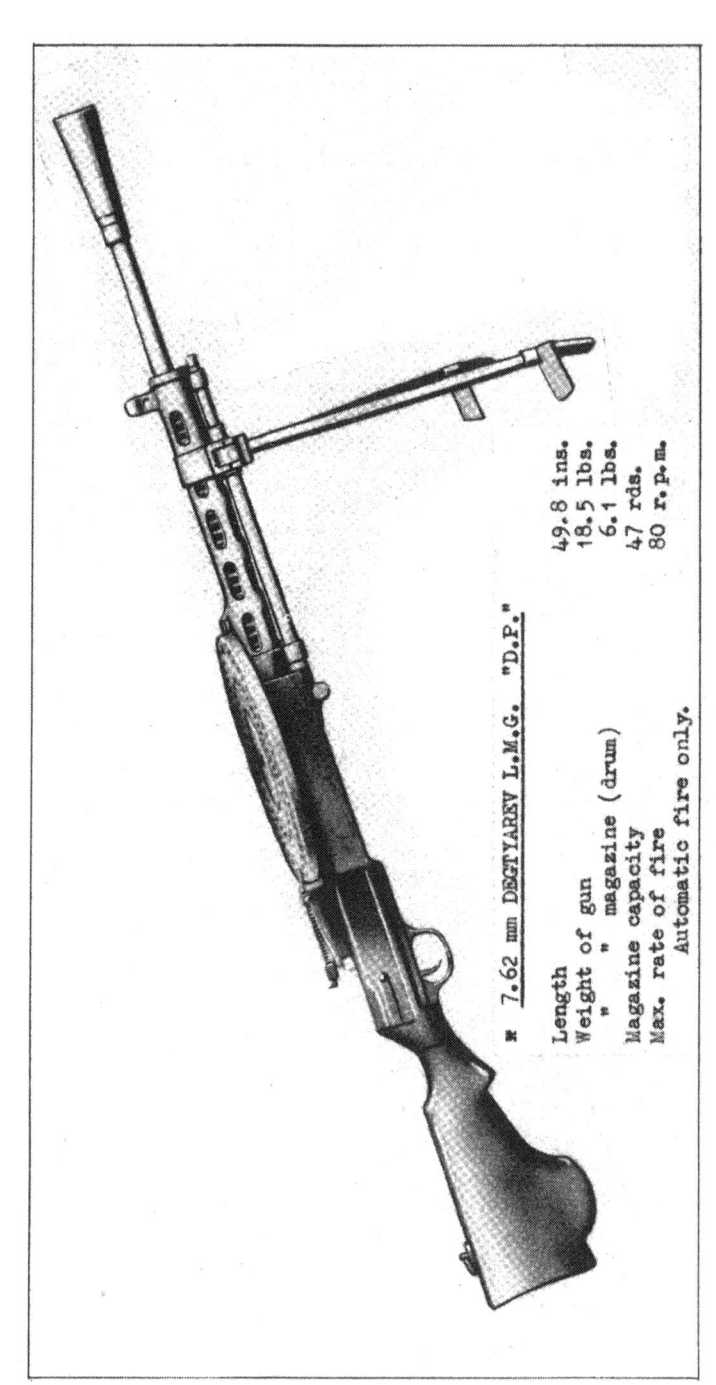

* 7.62 mm DEGTYAREV L.M.G. "D.P."

Length   49.8 ins.
Weight of gun   18.5 lbs.
  "   " magazine (drum)   6.1 lbs.
Magazine capacity   47 rds.
Max. rate of fire   80 r.p.m.
        Automatic fire only.

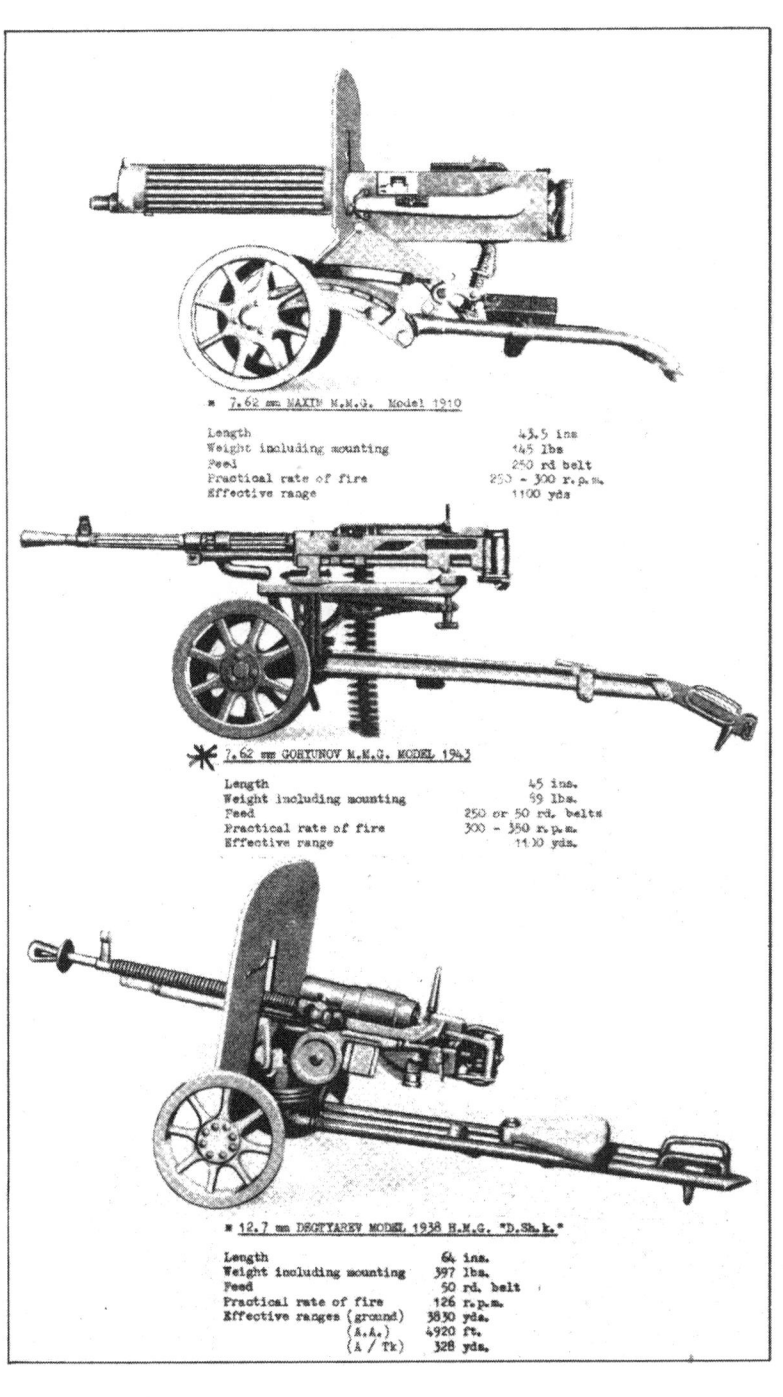

* 7.62 mm MAXIM M.M.G. Model 1910

Length	43.5 ins
Weight including mounting	145 lbs
Feed	250 rd belt
Practical rate of fire	250 - 300 r.p.m.
Effective range	1100 yds

* 7.62 mm GORYUNOV M.M.G. MODEL 1943

Length	45 ins.
Weight including mounting	99 lbs.
Feed	250 or 50 rd. belts
Practical rate of fire	300 - 350 r.p.m.
Effective range	1100 yds.

* 12.7 mm DEGTYAREV MODEL 1938 H.M.G. "D.Sh.k."

Length	64 ins.
Weight including mounting	397 lbs.
Feed	50 rd. belt
Practical rate of fire	126 r.p.m.
Effective ranges (ground)	3830 yds.
(A.A.)	4920 ft.
(A / Tk)	328 yds.

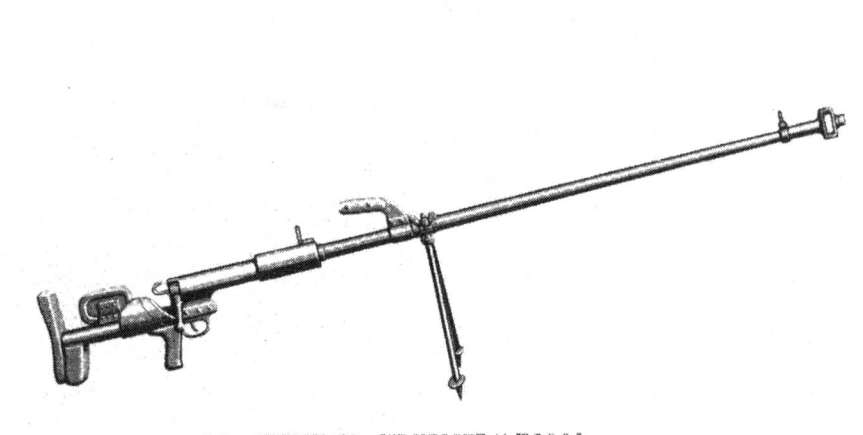

* 14.5 mm DEGTYAREV ANTI - TANK RIFLE MODEL 41 "P.T.R.D."

Length	79 ins.
Weight	38 lbs.
Feed	Single - loader
Effective range	550 yds.
Max. rate of fire	8 - 10 r.p.m.
Penetration	Penetrates 40 mm at Normal, at 300 yds. range.

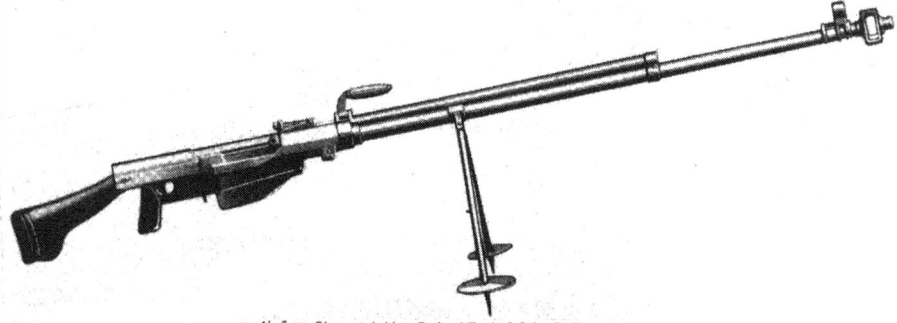

* 14.5 mm Simonov Anti - Tank rifle Model 41 "P.T.R.S."

Length	84 ins.
Weight	46 lbs.
Feed	5 rd. clip
Max. rate of fire	15 r.p.m.
Range & penetration as for "P.T.R.D."	

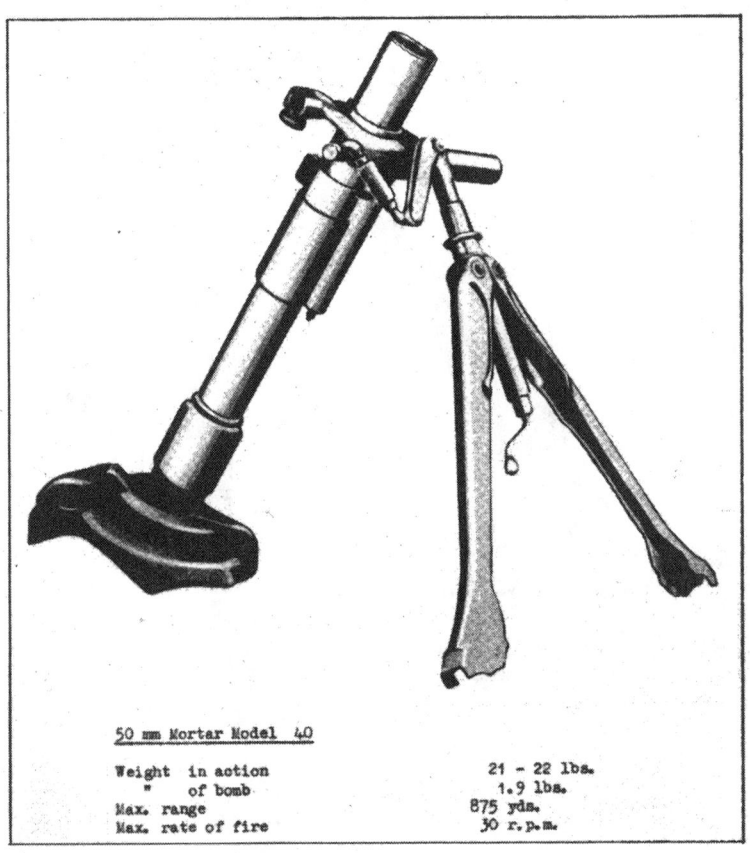

50 mm Mortar Model 40

Weight in action   21 - 22 lbs.
" of bomb   1.9 lbs.
Max. range   875 yds.
Max. rate of fire   30 r.p.m.

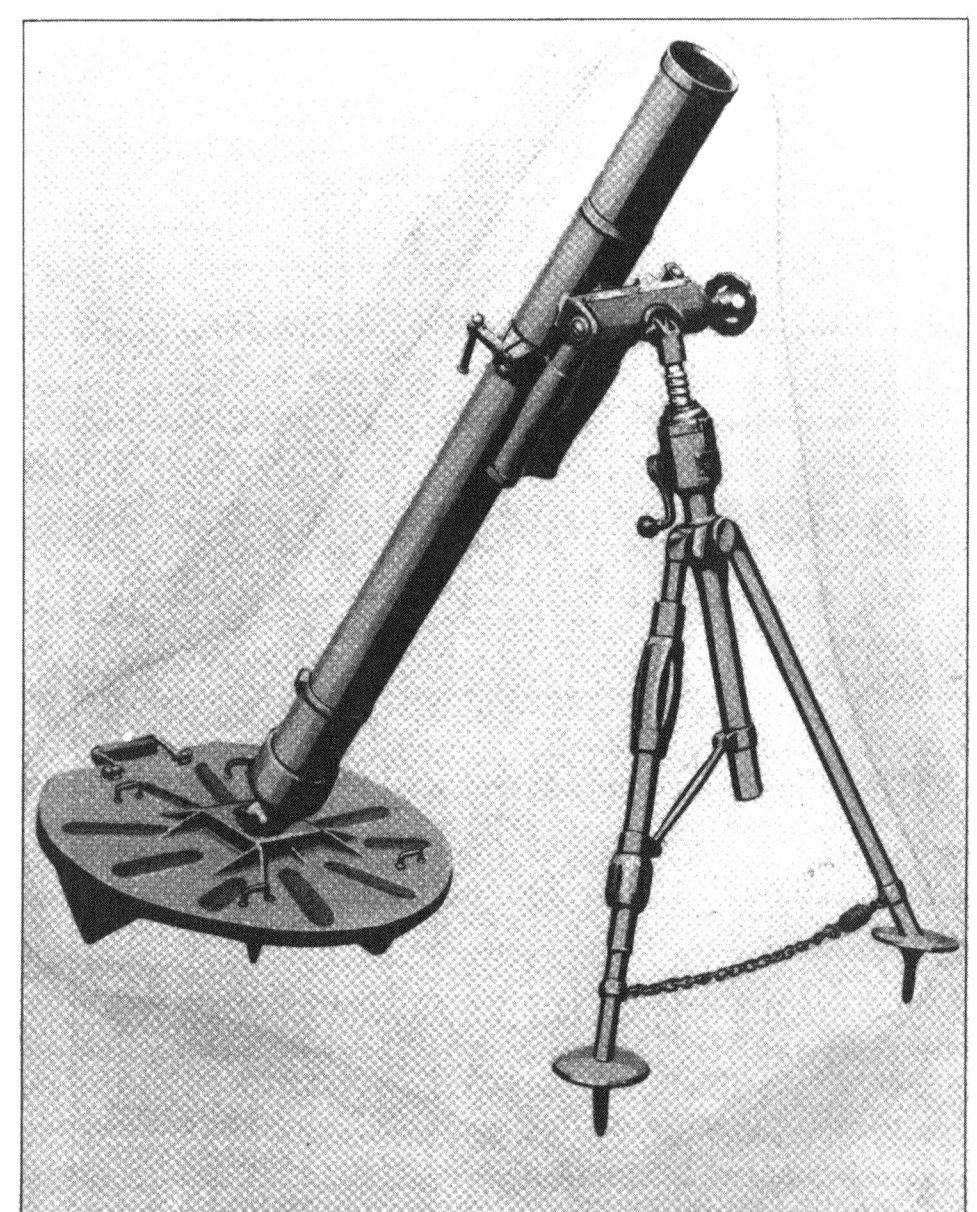

* <u>82 mm Mortar Model 37</u>

Weight in action	123 lbs.
" of bomb	7 lbs.
Range	75 - 3400 yds.
Max rate of fire	25 r.p.m.

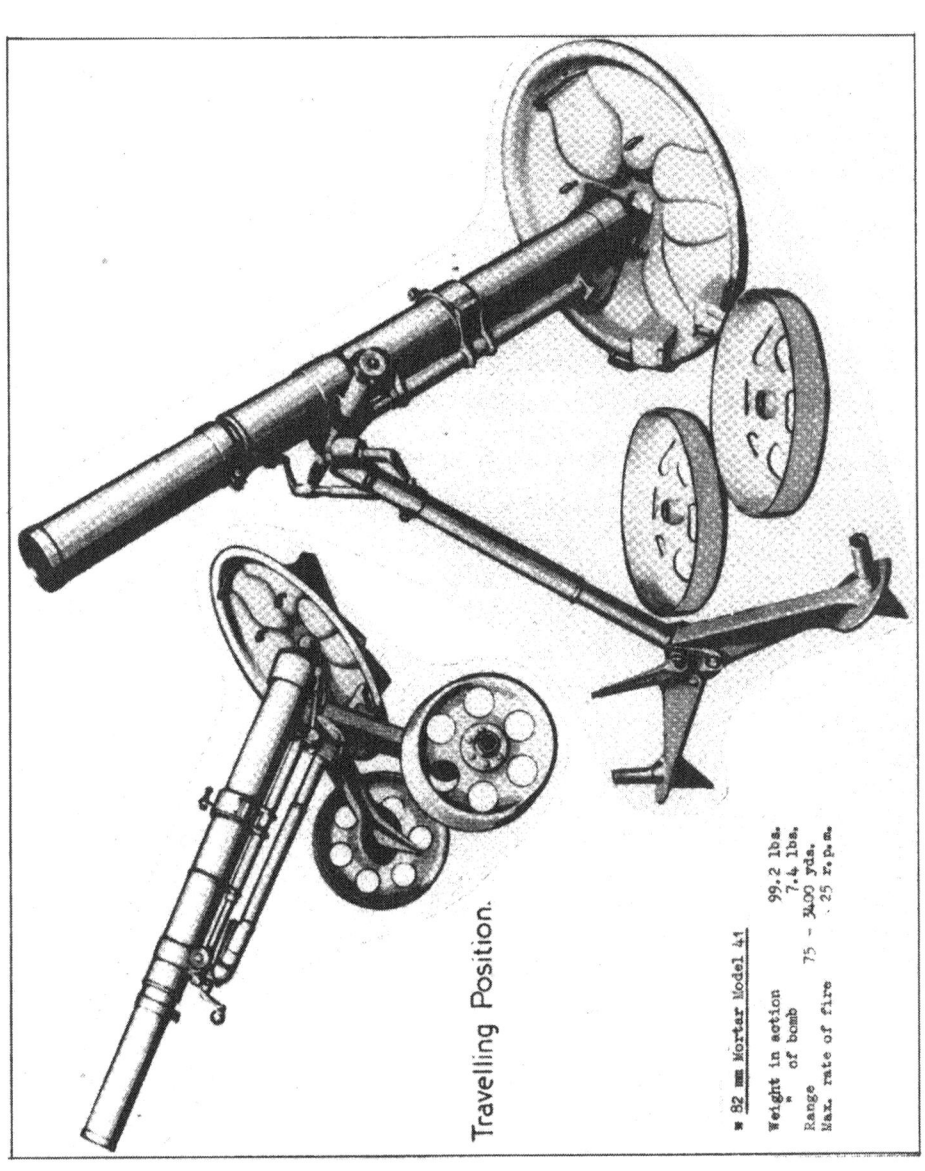

Travelling Position.

* 82 mm Mortar Model 41

Weight in action	99.2 lbs.
" of bomb	7.4 lbs.
Range	75 - 3400 yds.
Max. rate of fire	25 r.p.m.

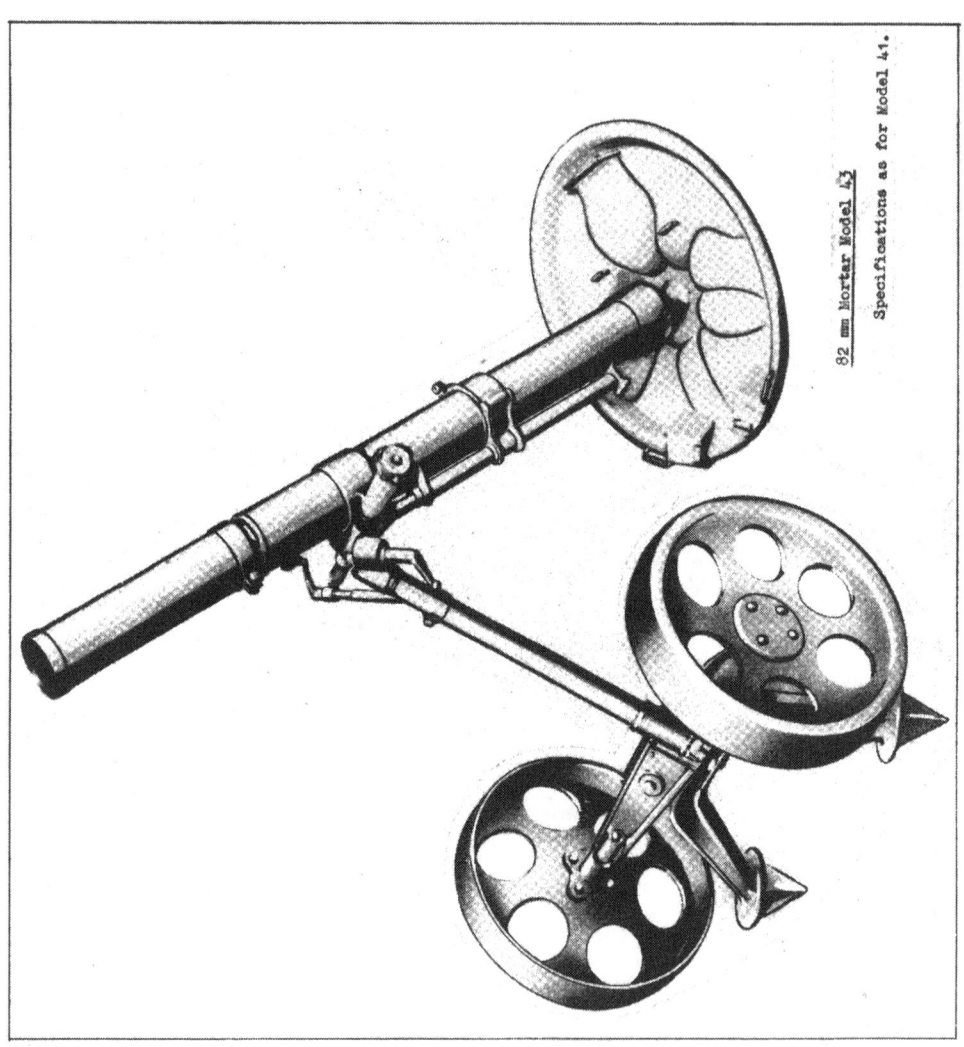

82 mm Mortar Model 43
Specifications as for Model 41.

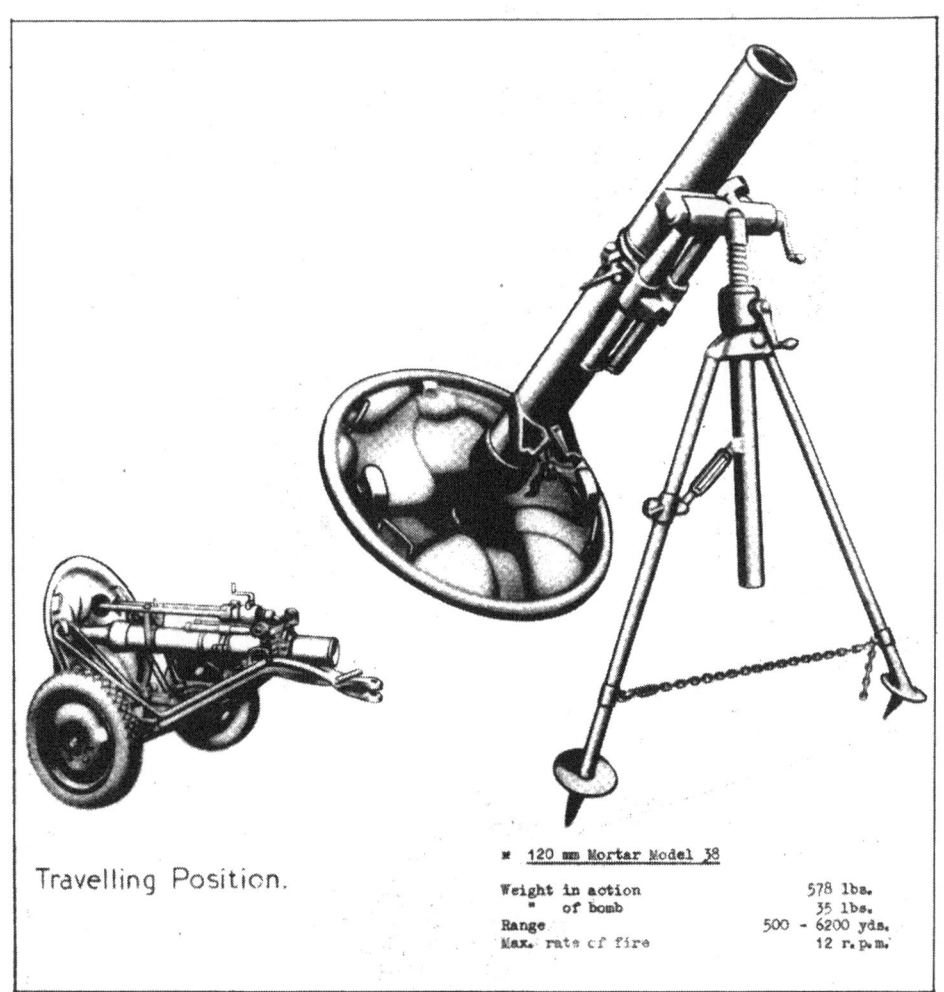

Travelling Position.

120 mm Mortar Model 38

Weight in action	578 lbs.
" of bomb	35 lbs.
Range	500 - 6200 yds.
Max. rate of fire	12 r.p.m.

ANTI - PERSONNEL HAND GRENADE Model 14/30

Weight with fragmentation jacket	1.8 lbs.
" without fragmentation jacket	1.3 lbs.
Length	9.3 ins.
Delay	3.5 - 5 secs.

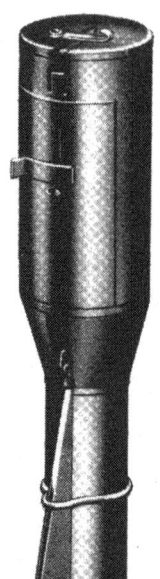

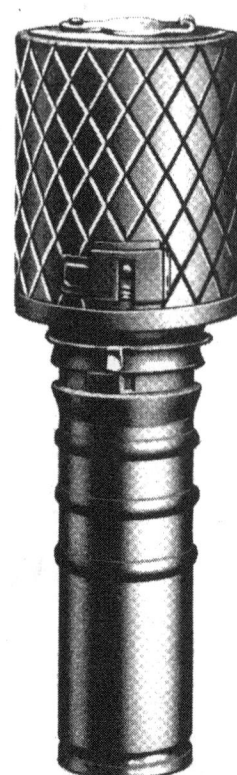

ANTI - PERSONNEL "R.G.D." Hand Grenade Model 33

Weight with fragmentation jacket	1.7 lbs.
" without " "	1.1 lbs.
Length	7.5 ins.
Delay	3.2 - 4 secs.

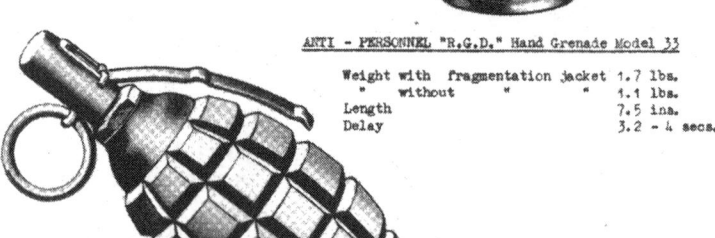

* ANTI - PERSONNEL "F.1." HAND GRENADE

Weight	1.25 lbs.
Length	4.6 ins.
Delay	3.5 - 4.5 secs.

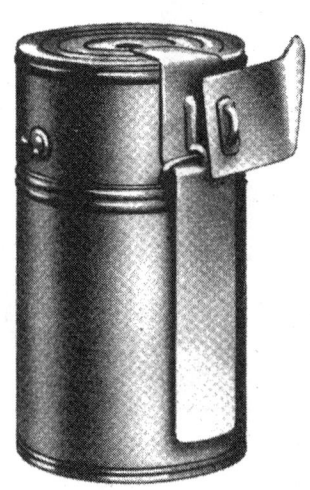

* ANTI - PERSONNEL "R.G." HAND GRENADE Model 41
  Weight   14 ozs.
  Delay   3.2 - 3.8 secs.

* ANTI - PERSONNEL "R.T.D." HAND GRENADE Model 42
  Weight   15 ozs.
  Length   4.6 ins.
  Delay   3 - 4.4 secs.

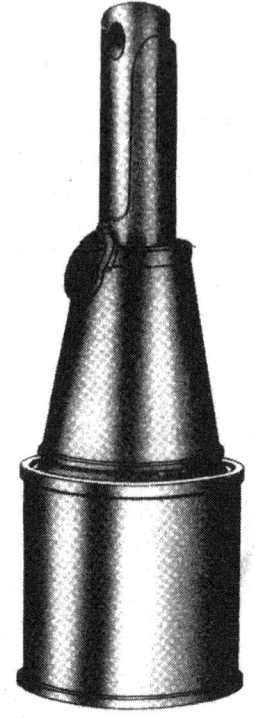

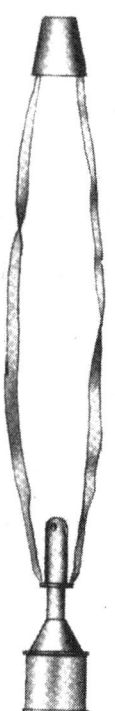

ANTI - VEHICLE "R.P.G." HAND GRENADE Model 40
Weight 2.7 lbs.
Length 7.9 ins.
A heavy impact-fused HE grenade for throwing against soft-skinned vehicles.

* ANTI - TANK "R.P.G." HAND GRENADE Model 43
Weight 2.7 lbs.
Penetration 3 ins.
A hollow - charge grenade for throwing against tanks.

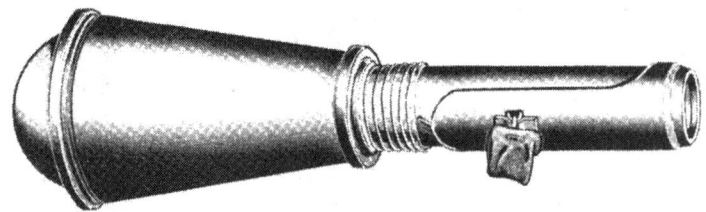

ANTI - TANK "R.P.G. 6" HAND GRENADE
Weight 2.5 lbs.
Penetration 3 ins.

A hollow-charge grenade for throwing against tanks.

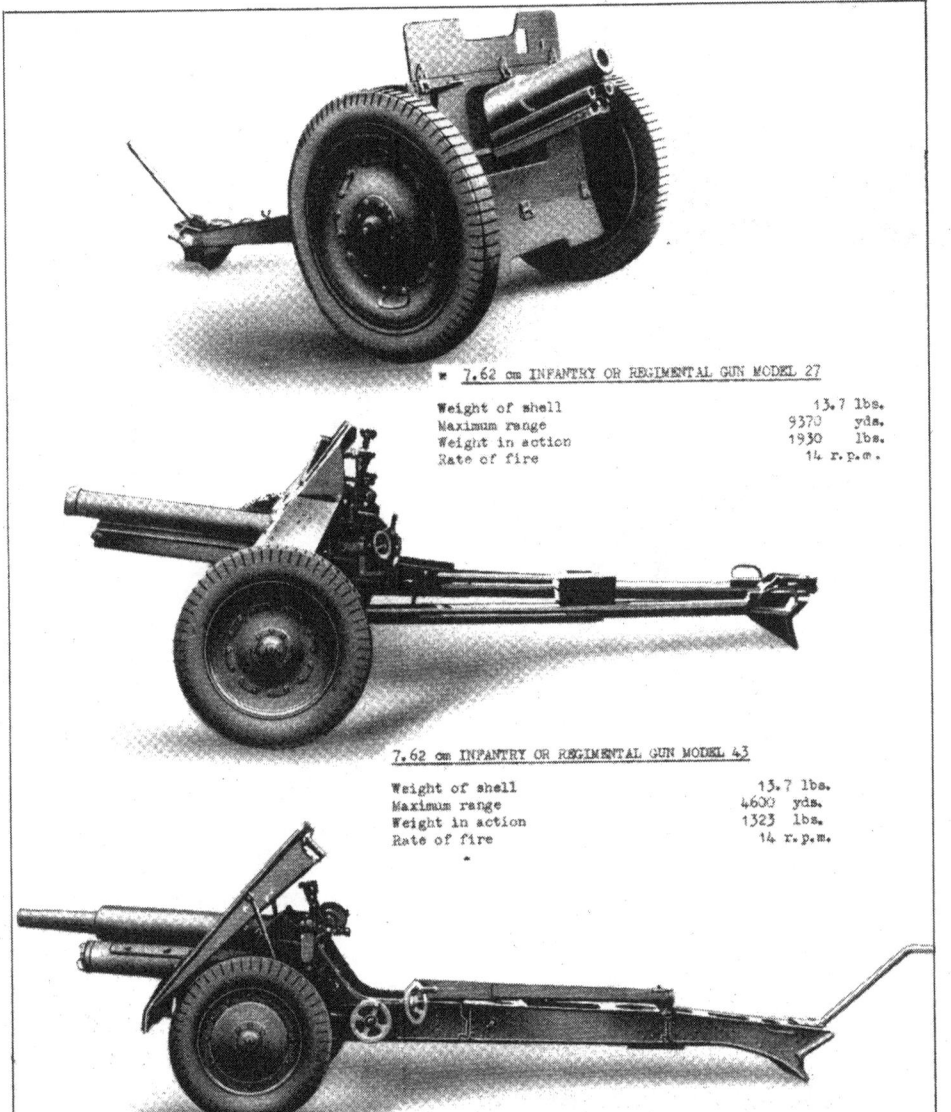

7.62 cm INFANTRY OR REGIMENTAL GUN MODEL 27

Weight of shell	13.7 lbs.
Maximum range	9370 yds.
Weight in action	1930 lbs.
Rate of fire	14 r.p.m.

7.62 cm INFANTRY OR REGIMENTAL GUN MODEL 43

Weight of shell	13.7 lbs.
Maximum range	4600 yds.
Weight in action	1323 lbs.
Rate of fire	14 r.p.m.

7.62 cm MOUNTAIN GUN, MODEL 38

Weight of shell	13.7 lbs.
Maximum	11050 yds.
Rate of fire	14 r.p.m.
Number of loads	10
Weight in action	1727 lbs.

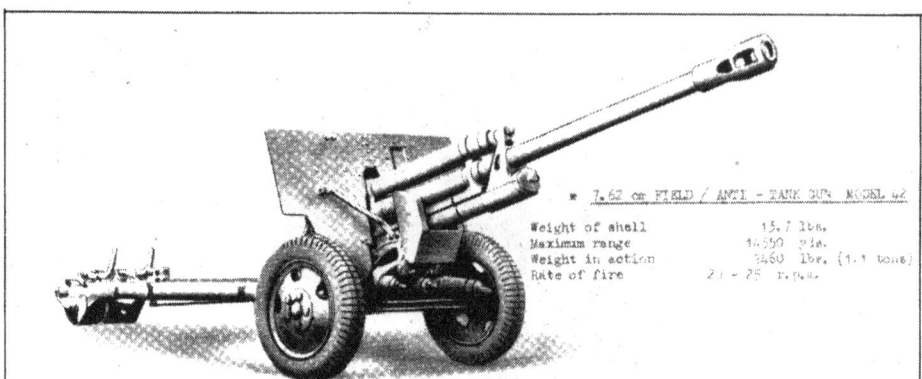

7.62 cm FIELD / ANTI - TANK GUN MODEL 42

Weight of shell   15.7 lbs.
Maximum range   14550 yds.
Weight in action   2460 lbs. (1.1 tons)
Rate of fire   20 - 25 r.p.m.

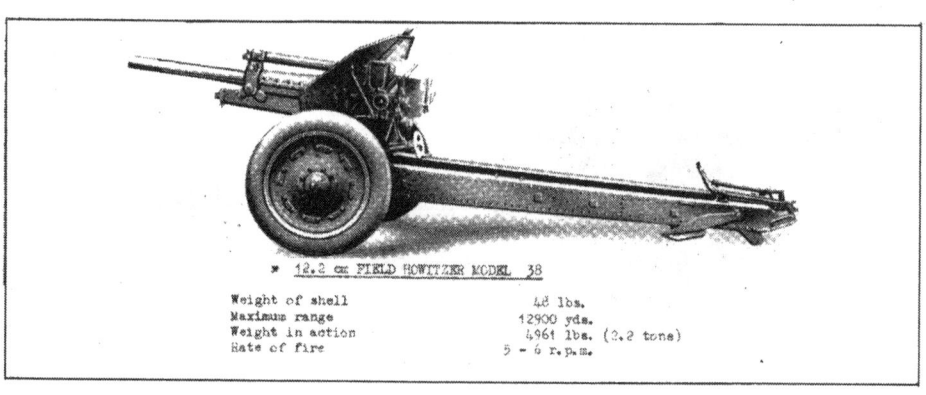

12.2 cm FIELD HOWITZER MODEL 38

Weight of shell   48 lbs.
Maximum range   12900 yds.
Weight in action   4961 lbs. (2.2 tons)
Rate of fire   5 - 6 r.p.m.

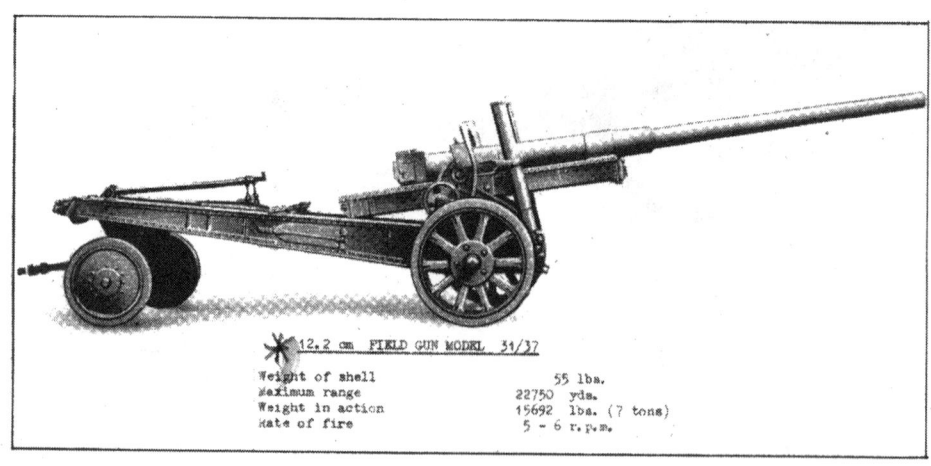

12.2 cm FIELD GUN MODEL 31/37

Weight of shell   55 lbs.
Maximum range   22750 yds.
Weight in action   15692 lbs. (7 tons)
Rate of fire   5 - 6 r.p.m.

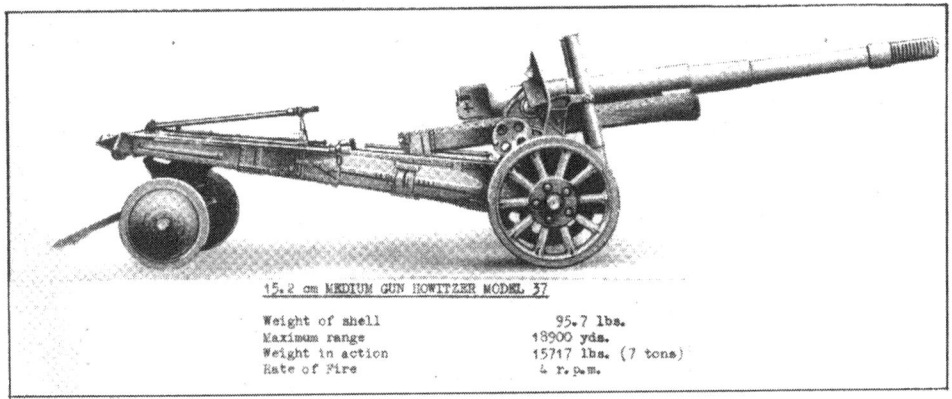

15.2 cm MEDIUM GUN HOWITZER MODEL 37

Weight of shell	95.7 lbs.
Maximum range	18900 yds.
Weight in action	15717 lbs. (7 tons)
Rate of Fire	4 r.p.m.

15.2 cm MEDIUM HOWITZER MODEL 38 ✱

Weight of shell	88 lbs.
Maximum range	13560 yds.
Weight in action	9151 lbs. (4.1 tons)
Rate of fire	4 r.p.m.

15.2 cm MEDIUM HOWITZER MODEL 43

Weight of shell	88 lbs.
Maximum range	13560 yds.
Weight in action	7938 lbs. (3.54 tons)
Rate of fire	4 r.p.m.

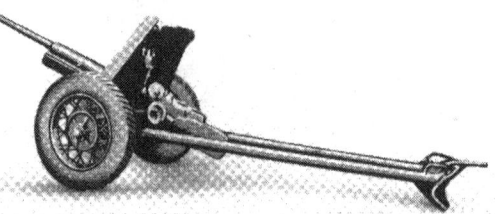

4.5 cm ANTI-TANK GUN MODELS 32 and 37

Weight of shell	3.15 lb.
Maximum range	8600 yds.
Weight in action	1235 lbs. (.55 tons)
Rate of Fire	25 to 30 r.p.m.

4.5 cm ANTI-TANK GUN MODEL 42

Weight of shell	3.15 lbs.
Maximum range	8750 yds.
Rate of fire	30 r.p.m.
Weight in action	1257 lbs. (.56 tons)

5.7 cm ANTI-TANK GUN MODEL 41

Weight of shell	6.9 lbs.
Maximum range	5690 yds.
Weight in action	2480 lbs. (1.1 tons)
Rate of fire	25 r.p.m.

5.7 cm ANTI - TANK GUN MODEL 43

Weight of shell	6.9 lbs.
Maximum range	9200 yds.
Weight in action	2535 lbs. (1.15 tons)
Rate of fire	25 r.p.m.

25 mm ANTI - AIRCRAFT GUN MODEL 40 (Twin guns)

Weight of Shell	0.63 lbs.
Maximum ceiling of burst	14,775 ft.
Maximum horizontal range	6550 yds.
Weight in action	2370 lbs. (1.05 tons)
Rate of fire	240 - 250 r.p.m.

* 37 mm ANTI - AIRCRAFT GUN MODEL 39

Weight of shell	1.61 lbs.
Maximum ceiling of burst	19680 ft.
Maximum horizontal range	8750 yds.
Weight in action	4410 lbs.
Rate of fire	160 - 180 r.p.m.

76 mm ANTI-AIRCRAFT GUN MODEL 38

Weight of shell	14.54 lbs.
Maximum ceiling of burst	31.170 ft.
Maximum horizontal range	15.650 yds.
Weight in action	9481 lbs.
Rate of fire	15-20 r.p.m.

85 mm ANTI-AIRCRAFT GUN MODEL 39

Weight of shell	20.2 lbs.
Maximum ceiling of burst	34500 ft.
Maximum horizontal range	16950 yds.
Weight in action	9482 lbs. (4.23 tons)
Rate of fire	15-20 r.p.m.

LIGHT TANK T.70

Weight   9.05 Tons   Crew 2

Armament   45 mm Gun   Maximum road speed   21 m.p.h.
1 Coax M.G.

MEDIUM TANK T 34

Weight   27.8 Tons   Crew 4

Armament   76.2 mm HV Gun.   Maximum road speed   34 m.p.h.
1 Coax MG
1 Hull MG

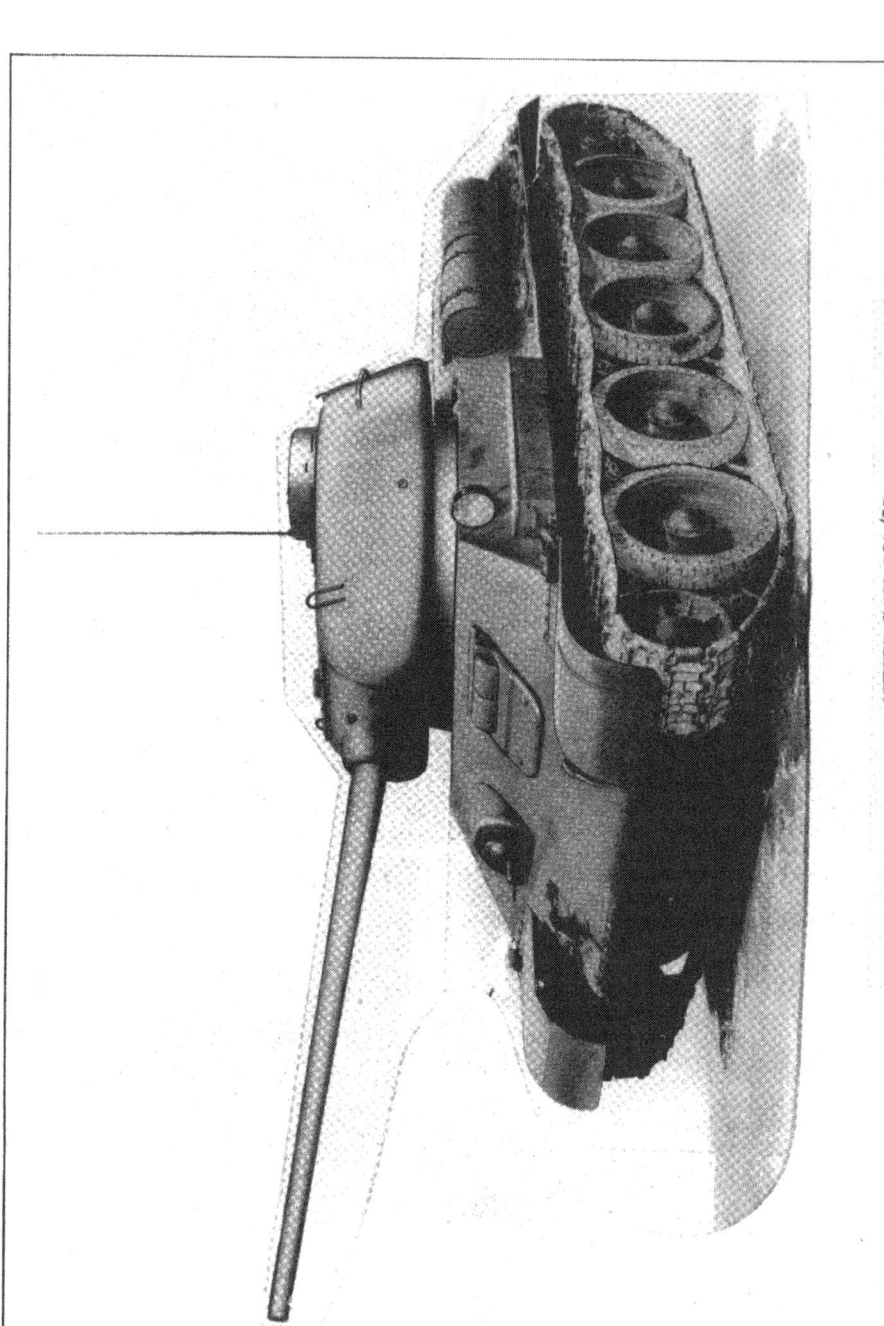

MEDIUM TANK T34/85

Weight   31.5 Tons   Crew 5

Armament   85 mm HV Gun.   Maximum road speed 34 m.p.h.
           1 Coax MG
           1 Hull MG

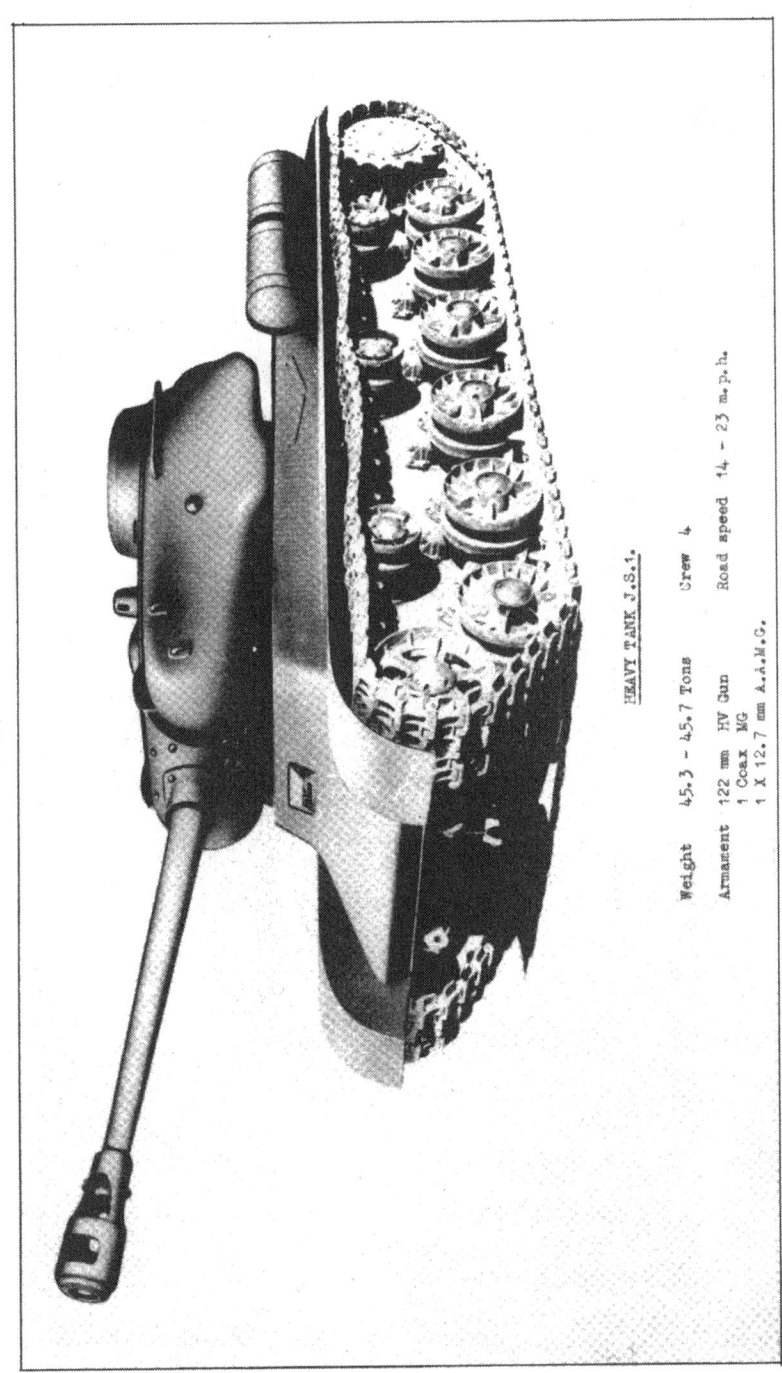

HEAVY TANK J.S.1.

Weight   45.3 - 45.7 Tons   Crew 4

Armament   122 mm HV Gun   Road speed 14 - 23 m.p.h.
          1 Coax MG
          1 X 12.7 mm A.A.M.G.

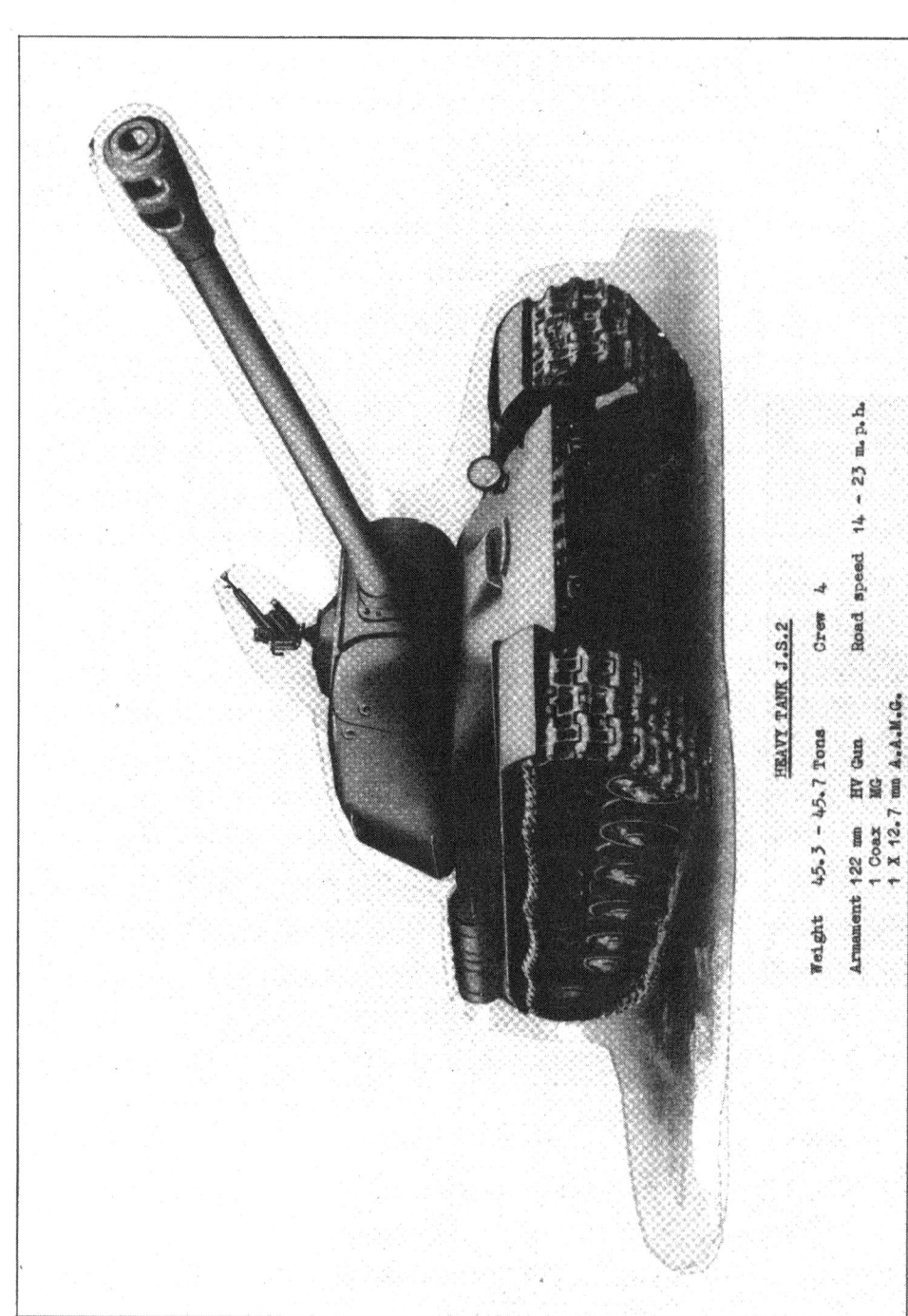

HEAVY TANK J.S.2

Weight 45.3 - 45.7 Tons   Crew 4

Armament 122 mm HV Gun   Road speed 14 - 23 m.p.h.
         1 Coax MG
         1 X 12.7 mm A.A.M.G.

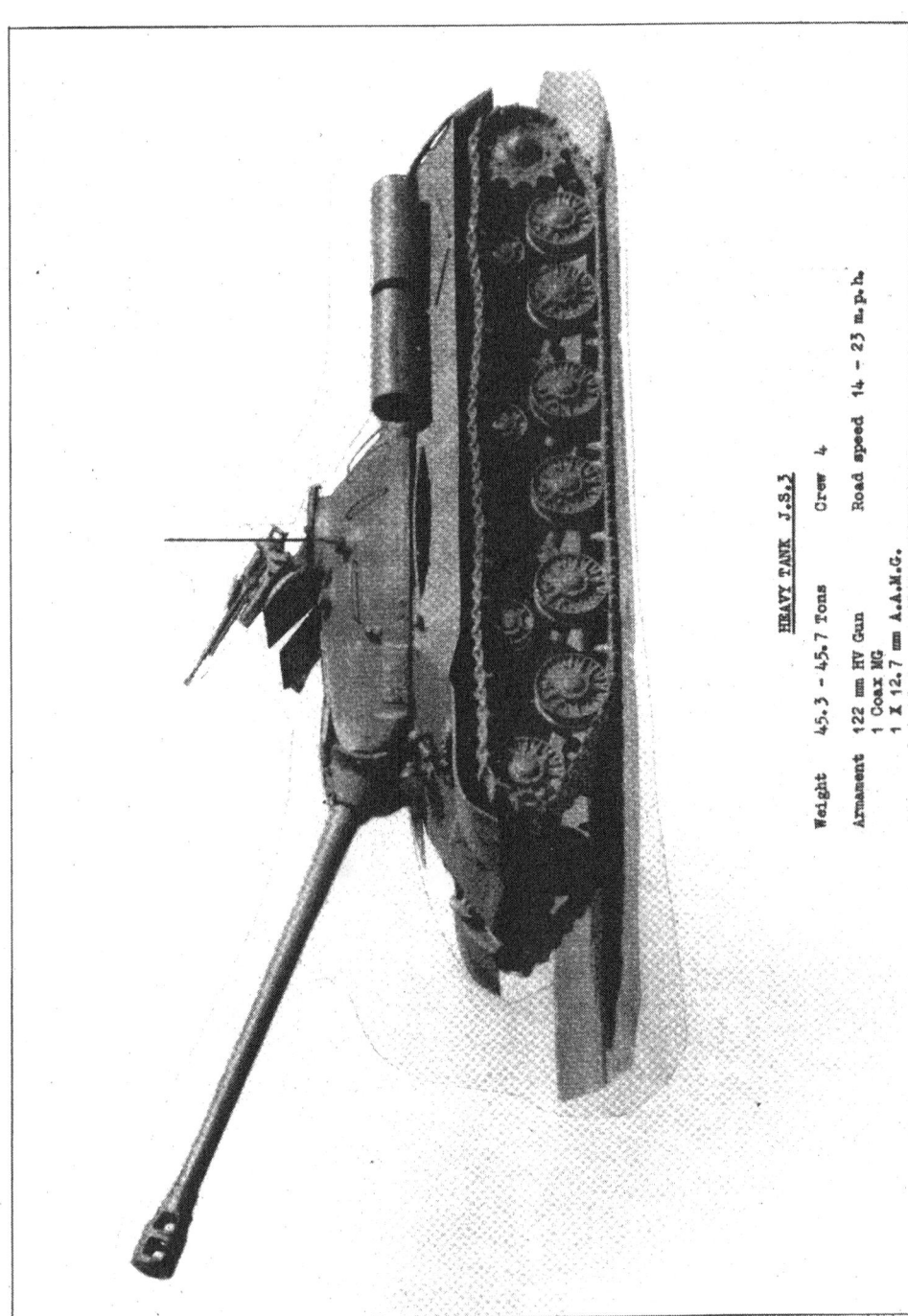

HEAVY TANK J.S.3

Weight   45.3 - 45.7 Tons   Crew 4

Armament 122 mm HV Gun   Road speed 14 - 23 m.p.h.
          1 Coax MG
          1 X 12.7 mm A.A.M.G.

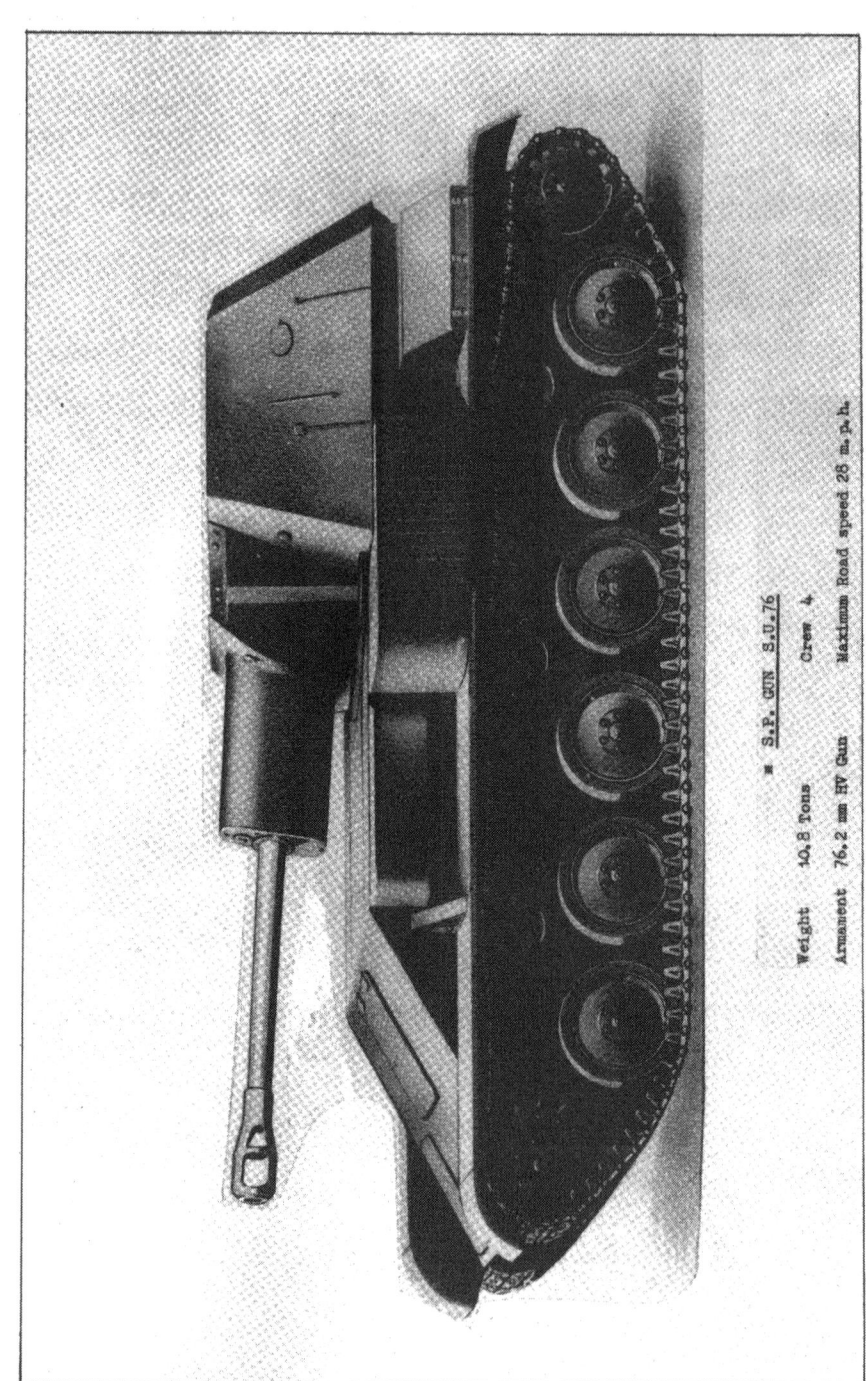

S.P. GUN S.U.76

Weight 10.8 Tons   Crew 4
Armament 76.2 mm HV Gun   Maximum Road speed 28 m.p.h.

S.P. GUN S.U. 85

Weight   29 Tons   Crew 5
Armament 85 mm HV Gun   Maximum Road Speed 34 m.p.h.

S.P. GUN S.U. 100

Weight   29.5 Tons   Crew 4
Armament 100 mm HV Gun   Maximum Road speed 34 m.p.h.

S.P. GUN J.S.U. 122

Weight 45.3 Tons   Crew 4 or 5

Armament 122 mm Field Gun   Road speed 14 - 23 m.p.h.
         1 X 12.7 mm AA Gun

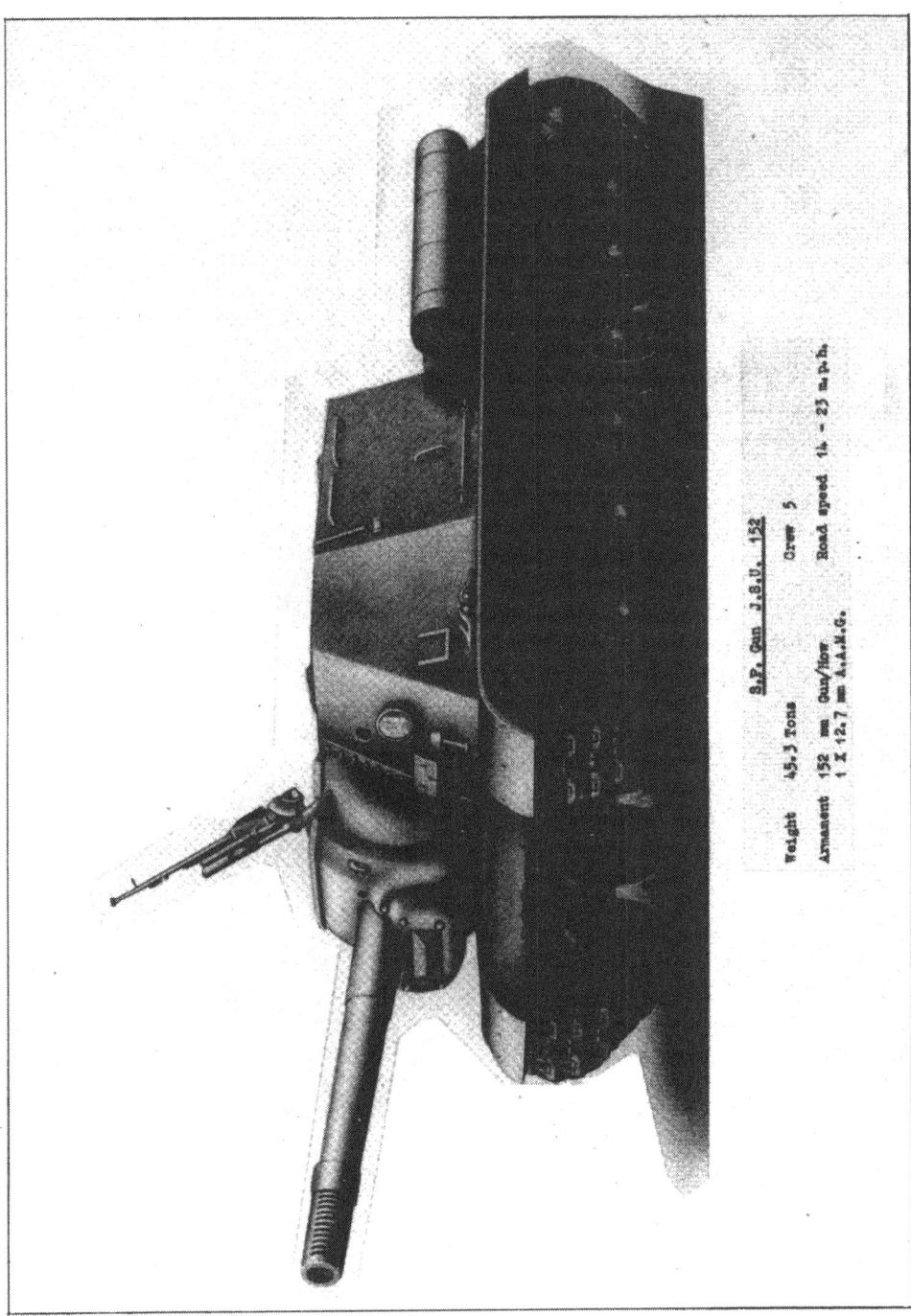

S.P. Gun J.S.U. 152

Weight	45.3 Tons	Crew 5
Armament	152 mm Gun/How	Road speed 14 - 23 m.p.h.
	1 X 12.7 mm A.A.M.G.	

ARMOURED CAR B.A. 10

Weight 5.17 Tons Crew 4

Armament 45 mm HV Gun Maximum Road Speed 34 m.p.h.
1 Coax MG
1 Hull MG

ARMOURED CAR B.d.A. 64

Weight 2.36 Tons   Crew 2   Maximum Road Speed 50 m.p.h.
Armament 7.62 mm MG

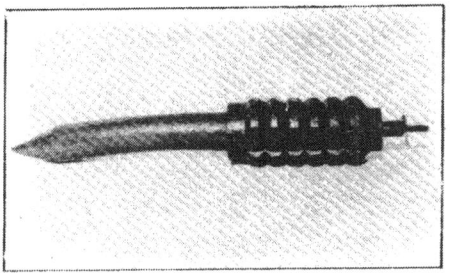

POMZ-2 Mine. This is a metal fragmentation anti-personnel mine, 7 ins. long, (excluding the stake) and operated by a trip-wire to the pin-withdrawal igniter.

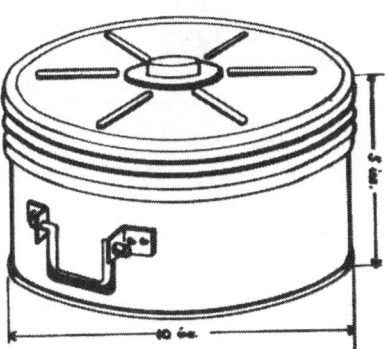

TM-41 Mine. This is a circular metallic mine containing 8.8 lbs. of explosive, and is operated by pressure on the ball-control igniter.

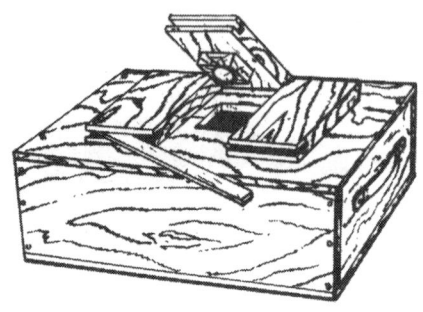

TMD-B Mine. This is a wooden locally produced type of mine, 11 ins. square, containing 10 lbs. of explosive and operated by pressure on a ball-control igniter.

Japanese Type 93 Mine. This is a circular metallic mine, 6.75 ins. in diameter, containing 3.25 lbs. of explosive. The igniter operates under a load of 200 lbs.

Japanese Type 3 Mine. This is a circular earthenware mine, 10.5 ins. in diameter, containing 6.6 lbs. of explosive. The igniter operates under a pressure of 22 lbs.

Japanese Hemispherical Anti-boat Mine Type 98. It contains 46.5 lbs. of explosive and the chemical igniter operates on impact.

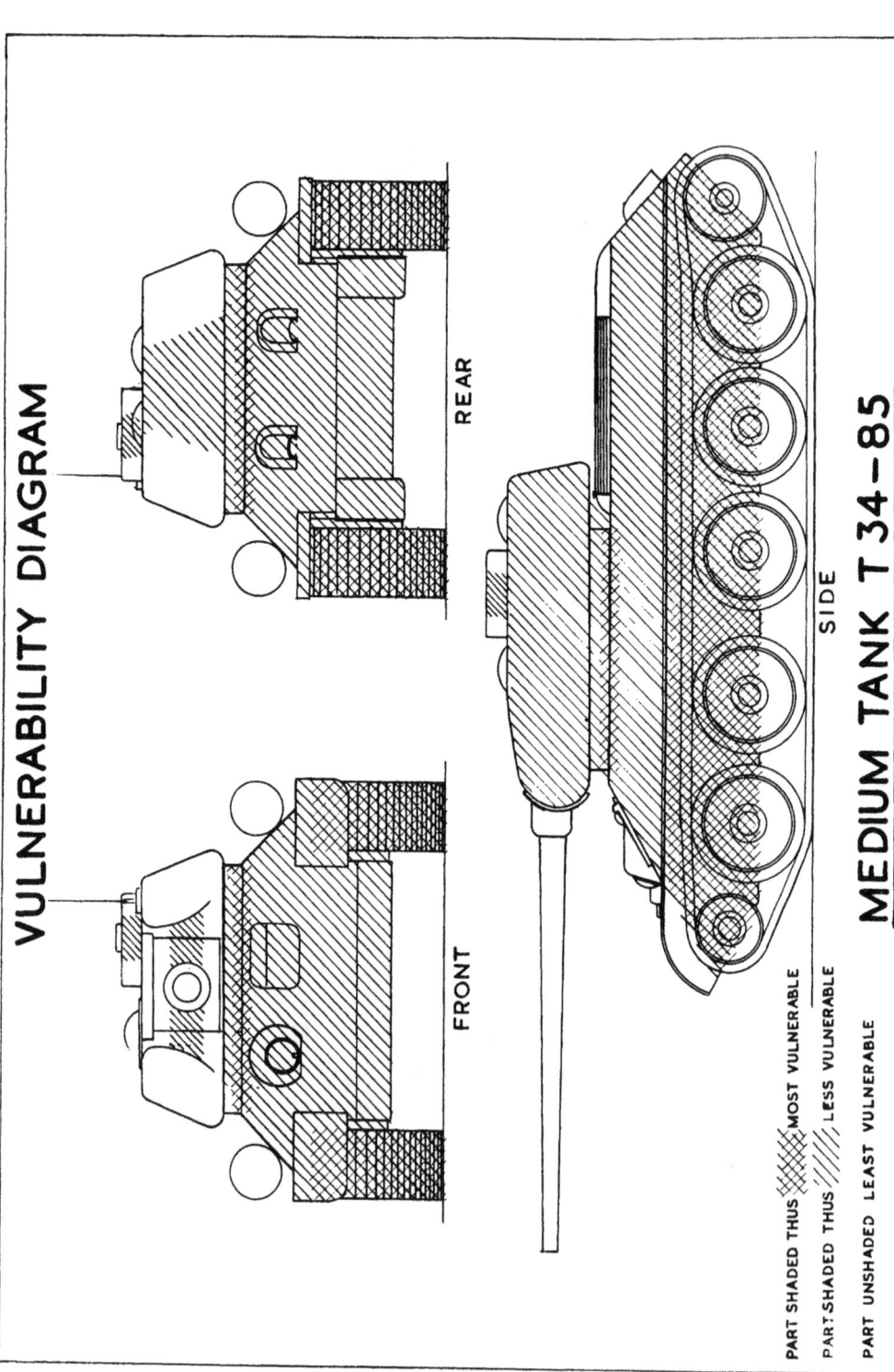

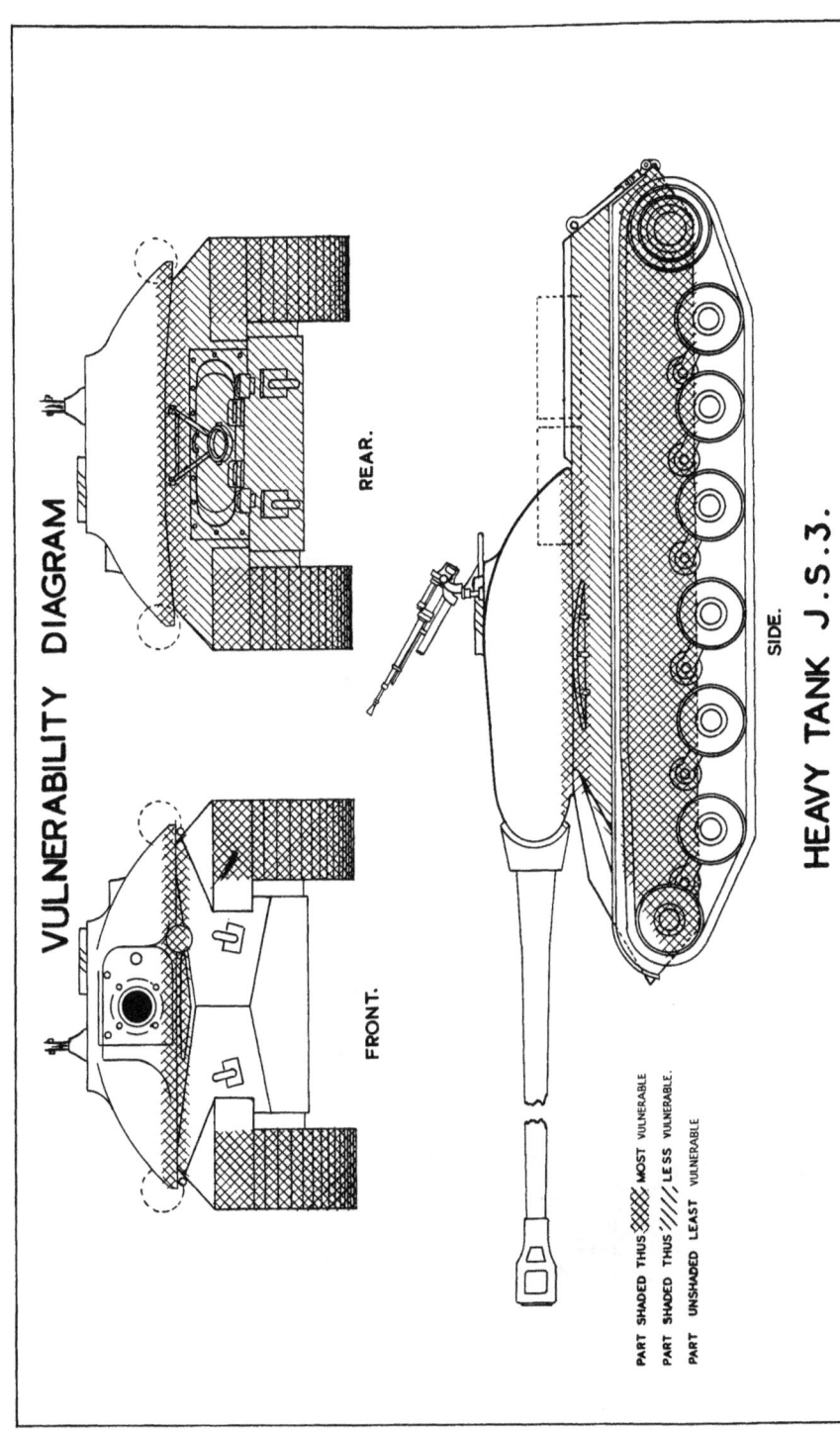

STOP PRESS

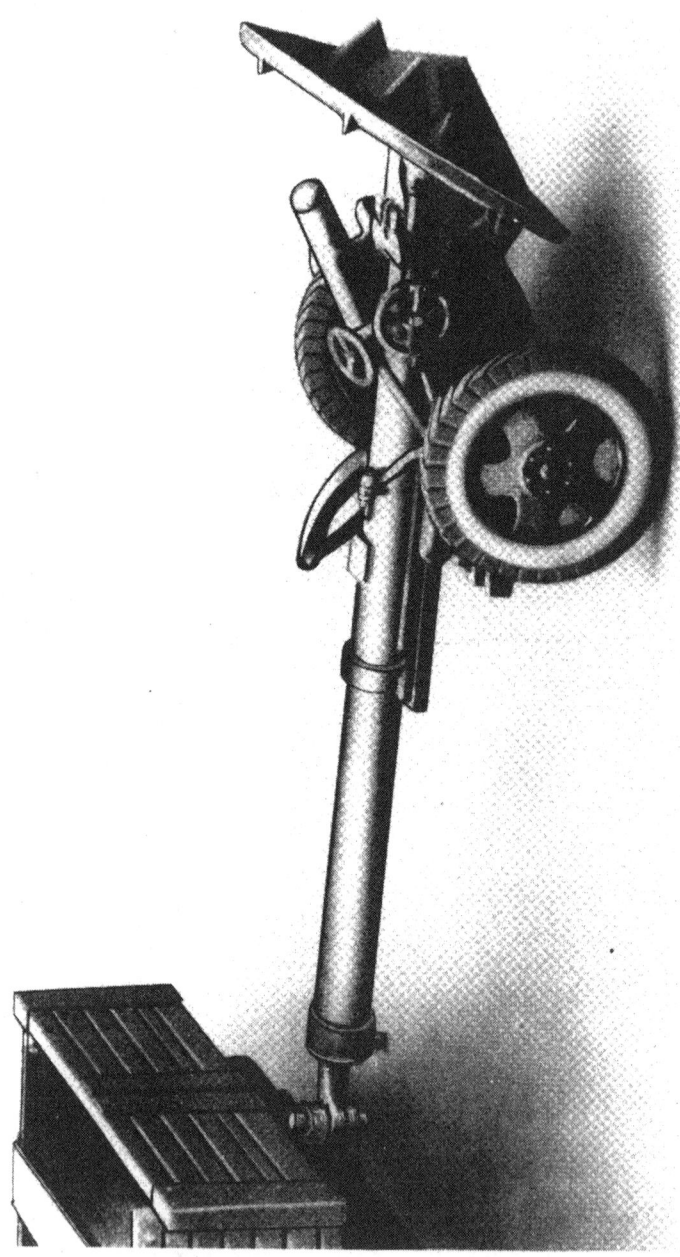

160 mm. Mortar M.43

Weight in action 2,380 lbs.
Weight of bomb   88 lbs.
Max. range   5,500 yds.
Rate of fire   3 r.p.m.

www.ingramcontent.com/pod-product-compliance
Lightning Source LLC
Chambersburg PA
CBHW061517040426
42450CB00008B/1660